LAUGH-OUT-LOUD JOKES

LAUGH-OUT-LOUD SPORTS JOKES

BY LEONA FOWLER

WINDMILL BOOKS

Published in 2026 by Windmill Books, an Imprint of Rosen Publishing
2544 Clinton St., Buffalo, NY 14224

First Edition

Editor: Caitie McAneney
Book Design: Claire Zimmermann

Photo Credits: Cover, p.1 (child) Sharomka/Shutterstock.com; series art (paper texture) OanaGherghe2/Shutterstock.com; series art (illustrations throughout) Look_Studio/Shutterstock.com; p. 5 Monkey Business Images/Shutterstock.com; pp. 7, 13 Lopolo/Shutterstock.com; p. 9 Prostock-studio/Shutterstock.com; p. 11 Denis Moskvinov/Shutterstock.com; p. 15 (left) Focus Pix/Shutterstock.com, (right) Studio Nut/Shutterstock.com; p. 17 Lucky Business/Shutterstock.com; p. 19 zieusin/Shutterstock.com; p. 21 A.RICARDO/Shutterstock.com.

Some of the images in this book illustrate individuals who are models. The depictions do not imply actual situations or events.

Library of Congress Cataloging-in-Publication Data

Names: Fowler, Leona.

Title: Sports jokes / Leona Fowler.
Description: Buffalo, NY : Windmill Books, 2026. | Series: Laugh-out-loud jokes | Includes glossary and index.
Identifiers: ISBN 9781538399255 (pbk.) | ISBN 9781538399262 (library bound) | ISBN 9781538399279 (ebook)
Subjects: LCSH: Sports--Juvenile humor. | Wit and humor, Juvenile.
Classification: LCC PN6231.S65 F69 2026 | DDC 818.'602--dc23

Manufactured in the United States of America

CPSIA Compliance Information: Batch #CSWM26. For further information, contact Rosen Publishing at 1-800-237-9932

CONTENTS

Words in the glossary appear in **bold** the first time they are used in the text.

PLAY BALL!

Who makes the best pancakes on the baseball team?

THE BATTER.

What did the glove say to the baseball?

"CATCH YOU LATER!"

What did the umpire say to the tiger?

"THREE STRIPES— YOU'RE OUT!"

Which animal is best at hitting home runs?

BATS.

FUN FACT!

Baseball umpires make the calls and **enforce** the rules in baseball games.

BASKETBALL BITS

Where did the point guard bring his date?

THE BASKET BALL.

Can you believe a basketball player's stories?

NO, THEY'RE TALL TALES.

Why can't you bring a basketball player to a nice restaurant?

THEY DRIBBLE ALL OVER.

Why was the duck kicked out of the basketball game?

FOWL PLAY.

FUN FACT!

Basketball has some of the tallest players in the world of sports. The tallest basketball player in the **NBA** was 7 feet 7 inches (2.3 m) tall!

SOCCER SHOTS

What's a soccer player's least favorite drink?

PENAL-TEA.

How can you tell a referee is having a good time?

HE WHISTLES WHILE HE WORKS.

Why did the soccer player use his hands?

HE WAS SICK OF DE-FEAT.

What position do ghosts play in soccer?

GHOUL KEEPER.

FUN FACT!

A soccer team can get a penalty kick when the other team commits a **foul.** They get a chance to kick the ball into the goal!

HANG TEN!

What do pro surfers do at work?

THEY HAVE BOARD MEETINGS.

Where do kids learn to surf?

BOARDING SCHOOL.

Why did the surfer cross the beach?

TO GET TO THE OTHER TIDE.

What did the surfer say to the wave?

"HAVE A SWELL TIME!"

FUN FACT!

Surfers often use longboards, which are longer than 8 feet (2.4 m), to ride waves comfortably. However, they may use shortboards for tricks and big waves.

FOOTBALL FUN

How did the octopus win the football game?

TEN TACKLES.

Why are punters likeable?

THEY ALWAYS PUT THEIR BEST FOOT FORWARD.

What did the ball say to the punter?

"I GET A KICK OUTTA YOU."

Why did the football coach go to the bank?

TO GET HIS QUARTERBACK.

FUN FACT!

Punters are football players who catch the snap and then kick the ball down the field for the **opposing** team to catch.

SILLY SWIMMERS

What did the elephants wear for their swim meet?

TRUNKS!

What did Cinderella wear to the pool?

HER GLASS FLIPPERS.

What's a sheep's favorite **stroke**?

THE BAAAA-CKSTROKE!

Why is Michael Phelps never late?

HE ARRIVES IN RECORD TIME!

FUN FACT!

Michael Phelps is a record-breaking swimmer with the most Olympic medals in history.

Michael Phelps

HILARIOUS HOCKEY

How do hockey players get to know one another?

THEY BREAK THE ICE!

What are hockey players and magicians both good at?

HAT TRICKS!

How can you pay a hockey player?

WITH A CHECK.

Where do hockey players get their money?

THE TOOTH FAIRY!

FUN FACT!

A hat trick in hockey is when a player makes three goals in one game.

WHO'S THERE?

Knock knock.
WHO'S THERE? Uriah.
URIAH WHO? Keep Uriah on the ball!

Knock knock.
WHO'S THERE? Meow.
MEOW WHO? Take meow to the ball game!

Knock knock.
WHO'S THERE?
Interrupting umpire.
INTERRUPTING UMPIRE WHO—?
—You're out!

FUN FACT!

The song "Take Me Out to the Ball Game" is often sung by the whole crowd at baseball games. This baseball **anthem** was written in 1908!

SPORTS WITH A TWIST

What do you get when you cross a sports star and a farm animal?

THE GOAT.

What kind of dog plays football?

A GOLDEN RECEIVER.

What do you call a bee with a bad hair day?

A FRIZZ-BEE.

What do you get when you cross a pig and a martial arts teacher?

A PORK CHOP.

FUN FACT!

GOAT stands for Greatest of All Time! Some sports GOATs include Simone Biles (gymnastics), Abby Wambach (soccer), and Michael Phelps (swim).

Simone Biles

GLOSSARY

anthem: A song declaring loyalty to a group, cause, or country.

check: A hockey move in which a defensive player uses their body to hit an offensive player to separate them from the puck.

dribble: In basketball, to move around the court while bouncing the ball on the floor; to let food or drink slip from the mouth.

enforce: To make sure people follow the rules or laws.

fowl: A kind of bird used for eggs or meat, such as chickens and turkeys.

foul: A penalty called for breaking rules.

martial arts: Any of several arts of combat and self-defense (such as karate and judo) that are widely practiced as a sport.

NBA: National Basketball Association, the men's professional basketball league in the United States.

opposing: Fighting or competing against another person or group.

point guard: The player who is responsible for directing a team's offensive play.

stroke: One of a series of repeated movements in swimming.

FOR MORE INFORMATION

BOOKS

James, Ryan. *Soccer*. Buffalo, NY: Norwood House Press, 2025.

Leatherland, Noah. *Baseball*. Buffalo, NY: PowerKids Press, 2025.

WEBSITES

Sports Jokes
www.ducksters.com/jokes/sports.php
Enjoy more sports jokes with Ducksters!

Weird But True! Sports
kids.nationalgeographic.com/weird-but-true/article/sports
Discover amazing and weird sports facts with National Geographic Kids!

Publisher's note to educators and parents: Our editors have carefully reviewed these websites to ensure that they are suitable for students. Many websites change frequently, however, and we cannot guarantee that a site's future contents will continue to meet our high standards of quality and educational value. Be advised that students should be closely supervised whenever they access the internet.

INDEX